We are all a
Beautiful
Mess

-We Are All A Beautiful Mess-

For my brother,
I am so glad you no longer have to do this alone.

-We Are All A Beautiful Mess-

Steve, Harry and Amber. Dan, Charlie and Timmy. Mum and dad. My grandparents who are no longer with us.

-With a special thanks to Ali, Paul and Gary.

-For all my muscular dystrophy friends and my tubie family, keep fighting the good fight.

True self-discovery begins where your comfort zone ends.
-Adam Braun

-We Are All A Beautiful Mess-

1. The Seeds of the Important Stuff

IT WASN'T SUPPOSED TO BE THIS WAY. I mean, I don't know how it was supposed to be, but it wasn't supposed to be this way. I found myself staring down at a letter, an A4 piece of paper that I had been waiting for for over four months to reach me. Every day watching and waiting for the postman to deliver something that could change my life forever.

I mean, who would have thought it? Your life, changing from the words written on a piece of paper. OK, perhaps you would have thought it – there are plenty of life changing things that are written on a piece of paper – but it just felt extremely surreal to be waiting to see if my fears were about to be confirmed by the postman. The poor guy. As it turned out, my life wasn't going back to the "normal" I had planned. I was going to have to figure out what indeed this meant for me.

How was this going to affect me, my body and my mental health? If that wasn't bad enough already, what about my kids, my working life? How the hell was my delicate brain going to navigate around this one?

It was a time I would rather forget, one that had left me completely deflated, emotional, restless and in a state of shock. At first I was relieved to have an answer after two years of fighting. Being told I would never have muscular dystrophy, being told it was anything and everything other than MD. But ultimately genetics and MRI results came through and confirmed what I had thought all along, I had limb-girdle muscular dystrophy 2A.

I was glad of the result because I was so tired and damaged emotionally from the fight to find out. The constant uphill battles, the lengthy hospital appointments, the invasive testing, probing questions, physio assessments, the looks of disbelief, the pat on the head while being turned away, the shrugging of shoulders, the "it will all get better for you".

Feeling dismissed right up until the point of genetic testing and still for a long time after that. I had to see someone to work through the damage. By someone I mean a psychotherapist and by damage I mean emotional. Because I will be honest, these experiences damn well stay with you. They don't just go away because you have an answer and for me it certainly was not a case of 'Right, got results, good, OK, thank you very much, let's get on with it.' I had to deal with the after-effects and sheer exhaustion from a fight I shouldn't have had to endure, and the challenge of coming to terms with having a new type of fight, one I would have for the rest of my life. Even writing this is extremely challenging. I don't think I can even put into words just how much damage it all did, but feeling totally let down and disregarded is a good start to explaining it I guess.

However, this book is not going to be about that story, for that is a story I am not going to tell. But it must be acknowledged. It is important, because it paved the way for this book and that is where this story begins: from those dark days, where the seeds of the important stuff grew. I wouldn't even be writing these words you are reading right now if that storm hadn't have taken place. The storm that left me dizzy and in a spin. That time was a time that created the start of a shift, such a seismic shift that only now is it so plain for me to see. It was a disguised shift in me so I didn't even know what was happening. At the time I couldn't feel it, visualise it, plan for it, so therefore I couldn't work with it. I was so preoccupied with what this disease was doing physically that I never even considered the positive power a life-changing storm can have on a person like me.

'2010' Pre-diagnosis commercial model days

-We Are All A Beautiful Mess-

The Seeds of the Important Stuff

I can't change the direction of the wind, but I can adjust my sails to always reach my destination.
- Jimmy Dean

-We Are All A Beautiful Mess-

2. Disabled

LIFE WITH A PROGRESSIVE ILLNESS IS SOMEWHAT OF A CHALLENGE. Just so you have an idea, things that you can do now you may find yourself struggling to do in a month's time, and your whole life revolves around coping with these ever-moving goal posts. For me, no longer working due to the progression of my condition, I found myself struggling to come to terms with the route my life had taken, which in my view was a complete nosedive.

All I seemed to be doing was trying to manage my daily pain and possibly get a wash and dress once a week. I would have been OK with it if I actually saw it as surviving for the time being, but to be honest I'm not sure I was even managing to come close to doing that. As time went on I realised just how depressed I had become. I really wasn't coping with any of this disabled stuff and I wasn't sure how much longer I could manage to breathe and wait for a resolution. My mental health was suffering greatly. Sometimes I found myself trying to imagine getting to a point in my life where I would feel content with who I was. I reminded myself that some people just never get there. As a person who was dealing with my mental health problems alongside my physical disabilities on a daily basis, I always had a heightened awareness when it came to the impact mental health can have on well-being. I was so tired of it all, I wanted to be rid of this struggle and I needed to find a way to feel better all round and to believe in myself again. I felt so incredibly low. When I started to search for answers, I realised that if I were to be completely honest with myself, one of the contributing factors for this low mood was that I felt unable to help other people like I once had in my working life. It still hurt having to leave my job and I was definitely still grieving from having to walk away from my position. It made me so incredibly sad because I loved to help people and I felt so useless not being able to do so anymore. I couldn't carry on like this. I wanted and needed to smile more for my children, my god they deserved it! I wanted to feel OK with all of these changes, somehow, because none of it was going to go away anytime soon. I knew the changes would keep coming; after all, it was a progressive disease.

As time went on and I lost more ability and my body became weaker, it really hit home that I needed to start making the most of life and embrace all that comes with it. It was the only way I was going to do this, it was the only way that made some sense to me. I needed to find some therapy, but I was so done with the drone of the therapists, done with the doctor's office. I was done with trying to explain myself and at the same time struggling to make any real sense of my feelings. I desperately craved and needed an outlet.

Days in bed.... sometimes months

Disabled

Without emotional content we make pictures; with it,
we create art.
- Gerald Brommer

-We Are All A Beautiful Mess-

3. Hello Strength ?

I HAD BEEN UP ALL NIGHT GRITTING MY TEETH. My hips hurt, my shoulders ached and I couldn't get comfy. This was the new normal for me, and good old sleep deprivation was most certainly keeping me company as I found myself once again in the kitchen, my power chair on tilt, a hot water bottle on my lap and a cup of tea on what seemed like a permanent refill.

It was 5.00AM and everyone was asleep. I decided I might as well stay up for a few more hours, hoping that after this time I would be ready to just fall into a deep sleep. I was feeling emotional, but too tired to cry, too exhausted to use any facial muscles (seriously - try crying with muscular dystrophy when it affects your face, I promise you the lactic burn experienced is truly not worth it!).

As I wheeled into my bathroom, I found myself drawn to the cracked tiles in the corner, thinking instantly how ironic it was that they beautifully summed up how I was feeling: broken. As I slid out of my chair and onto the floor, I knew I was done, I was so done with this battle and done with my life. I didn't know how I was going to go on. I sat there for a while, getting uncomfortable on the floor. I reached for my phone and swiped through my contacts. I swiped through again, and then another four times. I turned the screen off and placed the device down by my side. I removed all of my clothes and curled up as tight as I could manage, resting my head in my arms as if to hug myself for a moment. I was left wondering how the hell I was going to get back up. I decided to ignore that future issue as I reached for my phone once again. I scrolled through my apps and turned on the camera, resting the phone in my lap to look at myself. I stared at my face for a few moments trying to read my expression and I sat and looked at my fragile body, thinking my mind was in much the same shape.

While I felt scared, the fear didn't stop me, I felt it necessary to press 'capture'. I can't tell you why it felt necessary, but I will never forget that at that moment, it just did. With each snapshot saved, vulnerable moments were documented in sequence and before I knew it, raw emotion started pouring out of me, the pain, the worry, the sacrifices, the hurt.

As I finished I found myself looking through each image with mixed emotions but at the same time experiencing a real feeling of release. I stayed sitting on the floor with goose bumps on my skin, smudged mascara and red tearful eyes. I must have looked over the images a hundred times. They were to me so uncomfortable, so raw, so exposed, but fascinating. I stared, almost bewildered at what I had become. I started to see the capture of a melancholic strength, something I hadn't seen in myself before.

"Hello strength," I mumbled to myself, as I struggled clambering for my clothes. "I don't recognise you yet," I continued, "but good to see you are around." Looking back, I can say with conviction that this was one of the most powerful moments I have ever experienced. After some sleep, I realised I was at the start of something quite honest, quite beautiful. Creatively, for me, it was something quite different, something rather extraordinary! I had a disease which changed me daily. I felt it and it scared me, frustrated me, and I resented the fact it was forever changing me and making me feel so damned out of control. The feeling of lost control led me

to feel depressed and hopeless a lot of the time. I started to wonder, would this be

the start of creating some hope for myself again?

First set of phone captures at 5am.

Hello Strength?

-We Are All A Beautiful Mess-

Hello Strength?

Vulnerability is the birthplace of innovation,
creativity and change.
Courage starts with showing up
and letting ourselves be seen.
Vulnerability sounds like truth and feels like courage.
Truth and courage aren't always comfortable,
but they're never weakness.

-Brené Brown

-We Are All A Beautiful Mess-

4. A Therapeutic Approach

I HAD TAKEN PHOTOGRAPHS FOR QUITE SOME TIME PRIOR, portraits of other people's faces, mainly. I dabbled in classic portraiture, beauty and sometimes fashion photography. I had also taken self-portraits, but very much kept my clothes on and produced my shots all in the same style.

These new captures though were very different. I don't mind admitting, by the time I took the first photograph of myself in this raw, melancholic state, I had become fed up with the routine of striving for perfection and I had been left feeling good and refreshed by the change. I used a beauty editing style whenever I used to take portraits of myself. Being a wheelchair-dependent disabled woman, anxiety and depression made me feel below standard. I felt I was no longer attractive, and I certainly didn't love myself enough, if at all at this time, because I didn't allow myself to. I looked at myself and I judged my appearance, and I also judged myself harshly for not coping emotionally.

I had an unhealthy relationship with my disabled body, but it was not as bad as the unhealthy relationship I had with myself. I constantly reminded myself of how I used to look and used to feel, and it was so very damaging and destructive. My feelings of self-loathing were starting to make an appearance. But these weren't new, I had struggled with them most of my life. Rationally I could understand why all of those feelings were surfacing for me now. What wasn't so rational was when I then looked at how other people were coping with similar situations, I was consta-

-nstantly left feeling that I was severely failing. Now, of course I know that this was a major misconception on my part and that many people struggle, many people have times in their life, disabled or not, when they struggle with themselves in so many ways and for so many reasons. So in my need to get myself moving forward and on a road to feeling more balanced, the 'creative therapy' as I called it, started.

The more photos I took of myself the more I started to feel some freedom. Then I coupled some of those self-portraits with my deepest and darkest feelings: I wrote verses, poems. I probably have my dad to thank for my poetry skills since he was forever writing songs when I was growing up, and as a kid I would sit in my room with a pen and paper and write till my heart's content. I would get the urge to write at any hour, take photos at any hour. If I was feeling it, I was documenting that feeling. If that meant a three in the morning photo session, then that is what happened. Words would flow, so much so I started thinking about posting some of my words online.

I became more aware all this was becoming a therapeutic approach, a creative release that I was becoming even more hungry for. I won't lie, it was intense and it wasn't easy, but it felt positive and I just knew I wanted to carry on. None of this was familiar to me, but here I was at my most vulnerable, showing my body to the world.

Phone captures - 'Down days'

The Wasting Game

I wonder what you see when you look at me.
Do you wonder if I am trapped or if I am free,
I wonder what you think of my scars and lines.
My fading muscles from a disease over time,
I wonder what you see when you look at me.
Look at my body and take it in,
Do you see someone with a womanly frame.
Covered in sadness from the wasting game,
Or do you see beauty, more than skin deep.
Something to treasure and something to keep.

Morning phone captures after a night of pain and tears.

A Therapeutic Approach

Deep souls & complicated minds are the most beautiful of them all.
-Unknown

-We Are All A Beautiful Mess-

5. Chasing the Light

AS TIME WENT ON AND I EXPERIENCED NEW CHALLENGES, more photos were taken. Hospital stays, progression, overcoming the anxiety and fear of adaptations while trying to get by in a world that, for the most part, was still not adapted enough to meet disabled people's needs.

When I had a bad day, tears would flow, and my writing would flow. When I had a good day, I celebrated that day by spending it with the people I hid away from on a bad day. I couldn't be sure, but I think I was starting to develop a style which was exciting to say the least. Most of my early works I consider my best to date. This is because when I felt something worth capturing, my mood was captured quickly, on the phone. It was more authentic in the production and post work because I only had to reach for my phone and 'chase the light'.

I realised I was starting to make a habit of this chasing light business, all around the lower level of my home. Every time I would see an opportunity to express my feelings I would be there, always dedicated to getting that raw material down. I found it refreshing and it started to have a positive impact on my mental health, and even when I physically felt at my worst, having a mind filled with creative ideas was a pleasurable experience, one that kept me focused on turning the personal struggle into something worthwhile.

I didn't have fancy equipment, I didn't have the space for it (or the wallet), so I improvised with props I already had. I remember one particular day I was stuck in bed and I desperately wanted to create. I had a vision in my mind already and the light from my bedroom window was just perfect. I wanted to shoot the photo from above, but there was no one in the house at the time to assist me with any kind of set up and I knew that along with the light, my energy wouldn't last all that long.

I got some hair ties from my bedside cabinet and looped them into one another to create a small elastic chain, and popped it over one side of the camera body and then looped it over the other. I reached for the remote to my ceiling track hoist and pulled it along using the remote to position it above me. I then lowered the transfer bar and attached the camera with the hair ties to the hoist before sending the pulley back up to the ceiling. This then provided me with the perfect framing for a set of photos from above. The results produced some of my most popular fine art portraits in my collection today. I remember panicking all the way through, capturing shots in precarious positions thinking "If this camera falls now, it will only result in one outcome - death by Sony!"

The more I looked back at myself on the screen, the more I started to befriend my ever-changing body. Sometimes I would capture such pain, such emotion, it left me wondering if perhaps it was too intense for others to view, or would it be misunderstood or not understood in any way at all? Would the pain within the pictures put people off? Would I end up isolating myself with my new-found release?

Then I remembered the importance of being real. In a world full of filters and sliders and "my life is perfect" captions posted all over social media, maybe my art would be useful, maybe this piece of work would be the voice that would help another person living through a similar situation.

I realised that whenever I made art, it would be subjective. When I started a project, I didn't know if other people would like it, I had no idea how any of this work would be received. That was why it was so damned important to first and foremost be creating solely for myself. If other people ended up liking my works and could get something from them that would help their life, then that was a bonus. But I would return to unhappiness extremely quickly if I started trying to make my art, my personal journey, my life – yes, my life – into a quest for the acceptance of others. I had spent most of my precious time already trying to gain the acceptance of others and I wasn't about to revert to that time or make my artwork for anyone else. If I did that, then the vision and story would be lost.

I have of course experienced people that didn't like what I do, they didn't like my story and felt uneasy about my self-portrait artwork. At first this unsettled me, really made me feel that I was possibly doing something wrong by putting my work out there to the masses. But then I realised that anyone who puts anything before the public is of course going to be met with some criticism, so I let myself feel emotion over it and forced myself to keep moving forward, and to not be put off. It was their right to not like my works, or even take the time to try to understand it; similarly it was my right to carry on creating, as I had a bigger picture to present. I didn't want to lose sight of why I had started this project, to be derailed by fear of being rejected by not even a handful of people who didn't know more or understand my reasons.

Those who don't get anything from my work are quite simply not my audience. That was the way I decided to view it. I have suffered severe anxiety all my life, the opinion of others can be so detrimental, I had to work really hard at not letting it break me. One thing that having a progressive disease has taught me is to do whatever I need to do, get on with my life and make the most of all opportunities. Anxious or not, I had to take that nervous energy and turn it into positivity and make it work for me. I was learning to express myself and feel comfortable, and over time it led me to discover something quite outstanding: I was starting to create for myself without fear! This was such an important achievement and a crucial step for me. It was personal growth and the tool I needed that would lead me to helping people once again.

To anyone unknowingly visiting the house and looking in that caught a glimpse, I can only apologise for the sight of the naked woman crawling and shuffling herself along the floor and from room to room to get into patches of light before they disappeared, looking quite a strange state at times no doubt! Only ever as an afterthought did I wonder if anyone had witnessed my photo-capturing moments. Once the burn to create and capture had simmered down, I would sometimes find myself smirking and giggling at the thought as I sat still naked with a cup of tea in my hand!

The hoist, camera and those hair ties.

'The Moth' and 'The Fall' taken from above using the hoist.

-We Are All A Beautiful Mess-

Chasing The Light

-We Are All A Beautiful Mess-

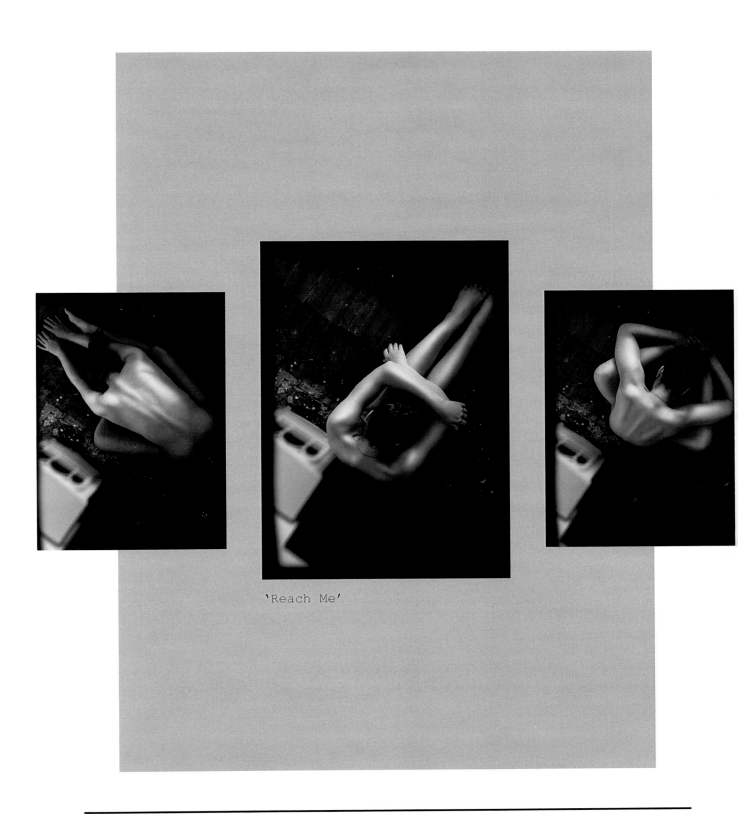

'Reach Me'

'Soul Searching'

-We Are All A Beautiful Mess-

'Dreams' - We all have dreams, the little things are often the biggest dreams of all.

‘Vulnerability’

-We Are All A Beautiful Mess-

'Tomorrow'

I just have this happy personality and a sad soul in one body.
It feels weird sometimes.
-Unknown

-We Are All A Beautiful Mess-

6. Carousel of Thoughts

I DIDN'T RECOGNISE MYSELF. WHO WAS THIS WOMAN? Continuing a project? Continuing to be inspired? Prior to this project and prior to diagnosis, I never continued projects. One of the reasons for that is I pretty much always ran out of steam, but there were other reasons that contributed to unfinished work; ideas remained just that and projects never materialised.

The truth is I ended up lacking self-belief, belief I could succeed in what I had set out to do. I lacked what I should have had in bucket loads, but my buckets were never full. I had always felt like a failure from a young age and I remember only dreaming about the things I wanted to do, never actually believing that if I put my mind to it and continued to spur myself on that I could indeed achieve what I wanted to in life. But for me, when growing up, achievement was only ever a dream. This feeling continued into my adult life, my life as a mother, my relationships with people close to me and even those not so close.

I always viewed everyone else as better and far more capable at success than I ever was. That in turn was reflected in my opinion of myself and therefore my ability to see myself as actually good at anything. This led to bad decisions, messy relationships, spiraling self-doubt, anxiety and deep depression, depression that made me so sad I can honestly say it felt as though I was constantly grieving. When I look back now, prior to diagnosis, in reality I realise I *was* achieving at life. I wouldn't have won mother of the year, but I was a good mum, with two healthy happy children. I took on a job, my first job after having kids, working in a nursing home. It was challenging, especially with my anxiety being at its peak, but I didn't give up, worked to the best of my ability and always gave 100 per cent.

I didn't always get it right and I certainly had days when I found everything overwhelming and I just wanted to run away from everyone, but I persevered. From being at home bringing up two children, to being thrown into a world so different was definitely a challenge and one I should give myself more credit for actually doing. I formed some lasting working relationships; in fact I still am in contact with those people today. So I was succeeding, but like I said, I never gave myself credit, I was just too unwell to see this clearly enough.

This job actually led me to a position in the NHS, a health care assistant in neurorehabilitation. I worked on a ward in a small community hospital and I really loved my job there, it gave me so much satisfaction. I was more stable in terms of managing my anxiety and even though I still struggled, I was prescribed medication which was definitely the right choice for me. I was becoming a little happier and therefore more confident, and it was here that, for a while, I started to believe I could possibly achieve much more, that I could work on developing my skills now my anxiety wouldn't get so much in the way of what I wanted to do: look after people. That is what I enjoyed doing so much, making a difference to people's lives in a positive way, being a part of their day when they needed to fight, helping when they needed to find their own strength, to witness people recover from such a challenging time, to assist and then celebrate when people reached their goals. To support them and perhaps hold their hand when they experience the flip side, to see them smile again is such an honour, one that even now years later has never left me. The feeling never goes. It was in this job I realised I may not naturally have had self-belief in bucket loads, but I sure had a lot of empathy with and belief in others. I think it is just within you, you either have it or you don't, and that is where my true happiness was. During this stage of my life I was diagnosed with bipolar affective disorder type 2, which in retrospect made a lot of sense to me.

I have always had what I like to call the "carousel of thoughts", a constant picture book of my life's past scenarios, projected and played on a constant repeat in my mind. The periods of heightened activity, heightened emotion, productive projects and housework full of hypomanic flare followed by the sudden drop into a deep ocean of dark-filled days, long bouts of rolling depression leaving me grieving and in a quiet and hidden despair. I always dreaded feeling good as I knew the darkness would be next and would last for sometimes months at a time. Sometimes the darkness would get so overpowering that I would take myself off to the doctor's office, for fear I would just never see the light again.

So, going back to my question: Who indeed was this woman? Continuing a project? Continuing to be inspired, continuing on? I can confess to you now, when I recall this, I didn't believe it could ever be, for the first time the inspiration had come from the person here writing this all down for you to read, and so I continued, I didn't stop, I didn't give up, I kept writing and taking photos, producing art with a story to tell. I was really starting to open up to myself whenever I got creative and it helped me both with those short hypomanic states and into those challenging long dark days. When I was creative with photography and penning my thoughts,

I found the dark days getting shorter, like the turn of the seasons from winter into spring, those dark days were my yesterday and my tomorrow started to become more and more a possibility full of light.

I started to appreciate my personal struggle, no matter how much I still argued with it. I appreciated that this struggle was valid, a massive part of my journey, one I could learn to work on a little more and one that I should not keep trying to dismiss.

'Royal'

Phone captures after 4 weeks of depression and anxiety

-We Are All A Beautiful Mess-

Carousel of Thoughts

Wrap Me Up

I woke all sleepy,
a sadness still inside.
Of last night's conversation,
fresh within my mind.
I am sorry that I hurt you,
and made you feel that way.
I don't want to make excuses,
I don't want to always say.
I am feeling rather guilty,
I am feeling quite unwell.
I did try to help myself,
I don't know if you can tell?
I am sorry that I shouted,
I was feeling rather weak.
I was feeling misunderstood,
I have been feeling this a while now,
I should learn to speak.
I don't like what it is doing to me,
I don't like what I become.
When I know that it is the culprit,
and I feel this disease has won.
I don't feel very good about myself,
right now I don't feel I am enough.
Please forgive me for acting out this way,
I get scared when it seems too tough.
The fear makes me crack my dear....
Please- wrap me up,
In your love.

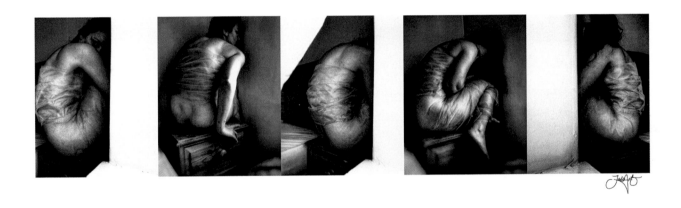

'Wrap Me Up' - Insecurities of bipolar

'Portrait'

-We Are All A Beautiful Mess-

slowly increasing a little in body confidence. Growing in acceptance at the same time I felt I was learning to create a space for myself where I felt freedom, where once upon a time I thought I had to rely on others to give me that freedom. I was working on becoming a little happier, whatever that was. I didn't always know. But producing art regularly gave me an epiphany: I could work on no longer being confined by anything in my mind, or defined by any element of my disease.

-We Are All A Beautiful Mess-

The Apology

I don't know how many times I have to tried to reach you,
To say what I feel and for you to hear it.
I don't know how many times I begged for forgiveness,
kneeling at your feet with a pain in my heart.
I don't know how many times I have left you feeling worthless,
but I am guessing it is far from a few and more like a lot.
I don't know how many times I have looked at you intensely,
and thought to myself, you are just not enough.
I don't know how many times I have sat on my own,
reminding myself of how much you have done for me-
to just turn right around and hurt you again.
I don't know how many times I have left you feeling useless,
defeated, unwanted and feeling alone-
With no one to turn to and nowhere to go.
I want to apologise for treating you badly,
I want to say it is the last time and I want this to change.
I want you to know that I love you deeply,
and I know you have carried me all of this way.
I am sorry I thought of you,
as ugly and aging, wasting and weak-
unattractive and ready for the scrap heap.
As I take a deep breath I look into the mirror,
I am ready to start loving you the way you deserve.

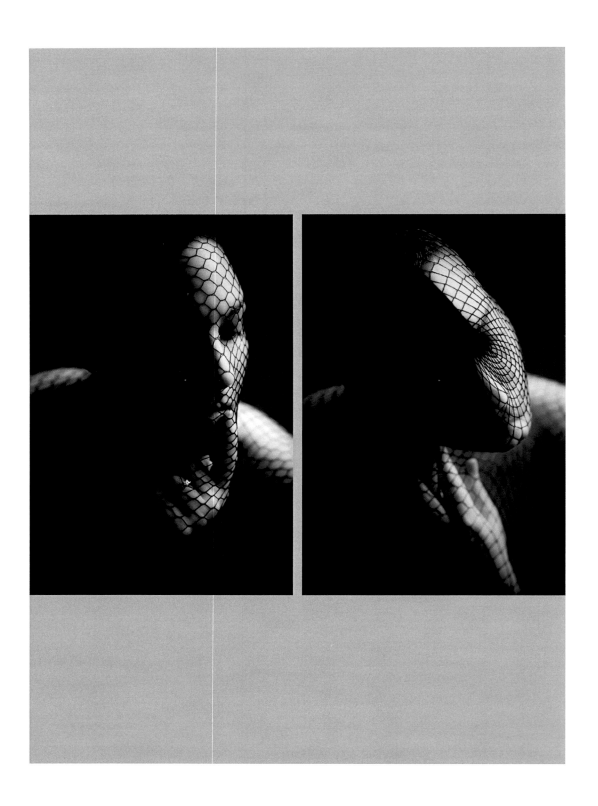

-We Are All A Beautiful Mess-

'Caught Up'

Every artist dips her brush into her own soul,
and paints her own truth into her pictures.
– Henry Ward Beecher

-We Are All A Beautiful Mess-

8. Weston and Woodman

EDWARD WESTON. FRANCESCA WOODMAN. I was beginning to hear these names mentioned a lot. At the time I wasn't familiar with these two photographers and at the time I had never seen their works, yet their names continued to keep cropping up whenever I shared a new piece of art. Feeling rather uneducated and a little embarrassed, I decided to do some much-needed research, and I am so pleased that I did.

When I looked at the work of Edward Weston, I could familiarise with the elements that made up his photographs using organic subject matter. His nudes for example, were never entirely exposed. Limbs slanted, hardly ever poised. The focus was not on obvious parts of the body but were a deliberate display of imperfections within the subject matter, showing the lumps and bumps, the curves and lines. Weston was what I like to call an "alternative cropper" someone who didn't stick to the classic photography rules.

Weston loved to work with dramatic lighting to produce photos of high contrast, to help highlight those imperfections that were such an integral part of his work. I really felt a connection with Weston's vision and the way each element he used had a key role to play. It sure did make my tummy flip when I realised I created my nude artwork in very much the same way. The feelings I experienced as I made this discovery, a rewarding moment of clarity washed over me which was an important part of my growth and one I am not likely to ever forget!

When I looked at the work of Francesca Woodman, this melancholic photographer had a profound effect on me. I felt I had made yet another important personal discovery when I read more about Woodman's background and her inspiration to create, so much so it actually haunted me for quite some time after. I felt an affinity with her, I could feel her pain, her fragility.

I immediately understood and could appreciate the emotional elements captured in her work. After all, I shared the same fundamental reason why she took photographs: to capture her mindset and how she felt right in that moment, something I understood extremely well. In my mind, she took me back to how I found myself on that early morning, feeling rather fragile, at rock bottom, on the bathroom floor taking self-portraits for the first time.

Woodman struggled with mental health issues from a young age and used photography as her creative outlet, producing black and white self-portraits, sometimes with a particularly haunting style. I found myself wanting so much to sit with this woman, to talk and to spend a little time with her. Woodman felt she couldn't go on and sadly lost her battle with depression, she committed suicide at the age of 22 in 1981.

I continued to get wonderful feedback from those in similar situations and fellow creatives, and as I was still struggling with my self-esteem it really helped me to keep faith in myself. With this extra boost I used this period to develop the side of my photography that I was perhaps, in the past, too cautious to show. I continued to concentrate on telling an honest story, and as I worked on this I in turn discovered more about my true self. Since learning Francesca Woodman's back story, along with my own story and those connections online, I now felt I had another strong reason to want to keep going with this project. I realised just how much it meant to me. I found myself wanting to pay tribute to everyone who struggled daily with complicated minds, who found they were perhaps only just treading water and who maybe needed some hope to keep them afloat. Through my writing and artwork I wanted so badly to tell them that they were not alone.

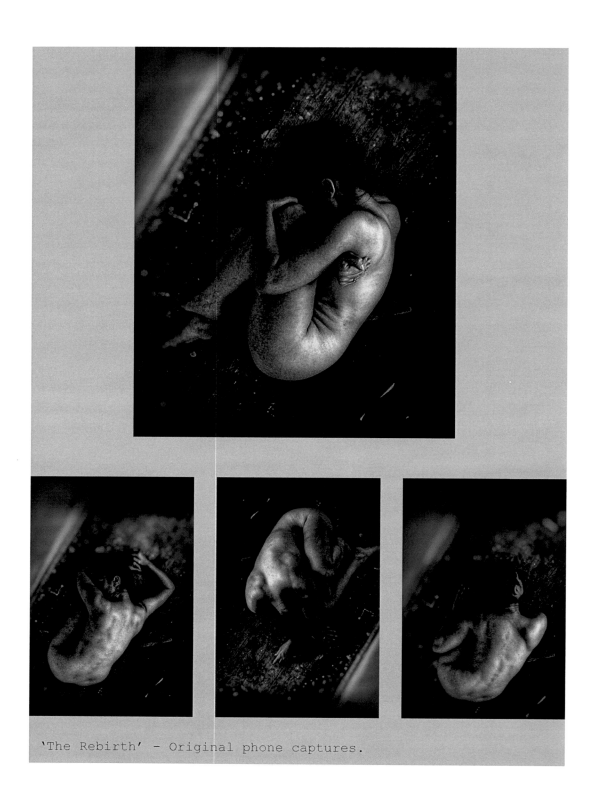

'The Rebirth' - Original phone captures.

-We Are All A Beautiful Mess-

'The Sitting Room'

-We Are All A Beautiful Mess-

'The Revolution'

Weston and Woodman

-We Are All A Beautiful Mess-

Weston and Woodman

Insta Filter

We have ups and downs, we are troubled, we are flawed.
We are vulnerable, we are in pain and we feel ignored.
Real life is not a set of pictures on your Insta with a filter.
Real life is when you look at yourself and try to find some kind of
peace within the mirror.
The reality we are taught is the plastic wrapped feature-
The eye catching beauty, the face tune-nice to meet ya.
We need to understand that when it all comes crumbling down-
We won't know how to love ourselves without a slider-to adjust our
superimposed crown.
Sometimes I may come across too down,
Too dark and too damn depressive.
Just because my everyday is not all fairy lights, rainbows
and 'perfect life' obsessive.
I want to show people that it is alright to be real.
To have bad days, ride out the storms and tell others how you feel.
To reach out and say it is OK,
To sometimes feel so tired of even living.
Many people feel like this,
I want to give you something real to hold onto & believe in.
You can feel struggle in your life-
have bad days and still be fucking winning.
So I will keep on posting, my reality for all to see.
There maybe someone out there,
Who is surviving just like me.

-We Are All A Beautiful Mess-

when I experience these things, when nothing makes sense to me anymore? It is inevitable, I may as well just be broken into pieces and swept up in a dusty heap to be binned. There was nothing I could do, nothing more I could say, as I sat there with a cannula in my arm, in the gastro-enterology ward, clutching at the damn bowl again.

I had a feeding tube fitted at the age of thirty-seven. I found out that the sensation I named 'The Spider', was actually the muscles in my oesophagus failing to contract in the correct order. They had become too weak, every time I tried to eat it resulted in being terribly sick because food and drink was just getting stuck in my throat.

I had a feeding tube fitted so I could feed directly into the stomach, allowing me to bypass my troublesome oesophagus. Unfortunately, this arrangement didn't work for long and it was shortly followed by gut dysmotility. Then my stomach decided to stop working too and so a few months later I had my tube extended which enabled me to get my nutrition fed directly into the small bowel. It was a period of time that required a lot of adjustment. Rapid change was something I had become accustomed to, but this change was by far one of the hardest. It was part of the progression of muscular dystrophy that I was never warned about, never prepared for and most definitely one of the biggest challenges associated with my condition, one I was really going to have trouble figuring out how to take on.

'Life Lines'

-We Are All A Beautiful Mess-

'Bipolar Dawn' -
Darkness is felt often but there will always be a dawn.

Art is to console those who are broken by life.
— Vincent Van Gogh

-We Are All A Beautiful Mess-

I feel so inconsolable,
But it is such a time wasting affair,
Knowing I am beating myself up,
and hurting those who care.

Being present takes practise,
Sometimes I wobble hard,
But the struggle I hope is one that's soon in the past.

Feeling these emotions I keep mostly deep inside,
This life is such a fucking crazy tormenting freaky ride.

I know that it is OK to feel lost and cry,
But I still feel guilty, when I want to curl up & hide.

One thing I have noticed,
When things get far too much,
The emotions bubble away,
I feel so out of touch,
When really it is just another shift in this part of a bigger story.
Acceptance inside is coming,
When you learn to put your trust in the journey.

'The Rebirth'-
Getting back up off the floor when depressed.

'White Rose'

I Miss You

-*We Are All A Beautiful Mess*-

I Miss You

-We Are All A Beautiful Mess-

'The Face of a Brave Woman' –
Exploration of what it means to be brave and the
misconception of what bravery looks like.

Bravery

Being brave is facing something head on even when you don't want to,
even when it is your last resort.
Even when you feel you don't have a choice,
you are crying out as you feel the terror like never before..

Being brave is taking a breath every day and keeping it going,
Being brave is when you manage to smile for a moment,
when feeling overcome with pain.

Being brave is screaming inside when no words come out ,
When there is nowhere to hide.
It is trusting in others to do the best for you,
As you hand over your life to them
Being brave is choosing to give the unknown a chance,
Choosing to stay here and choosing to live.
Being brave is falling apart, whilst holding onto hope.

-We Are All A Beautiful Mess-

Clothes scrunched up in a pile on the seat of my wheelchair, looking as messy as my rough and ready legs (which had suffered two months of hair growth), I could say without a doubt I was ready to go! (I could have successfully auditioned for a part in a Tim Burton film with those legs alone!) While laughing at myself in all my hairy, half asleep glory, I had no idea just how special this set would become.

"Electromagnetic" went on to be recognised by Vogue Italia and consequently was published in PhotoVogue. I guess the early bird really does catch the worm! Who would have thought those Tim Burton-worthy pins and a Pulp Fiction wig would get their five minutes of "strike a pose" fame?

VOGUE

'Electromagnetic'-
The spectrum of light we can see, and the light and power we
can't.

-We Are All A Beautiful Mess-

Electromagnetic

'Locked'

-We Are All A Beautiful Mess-

'Autumn'

-We Are All A Beautiful Mess-

'Solitude'

The worst thing about pain is that it is a lonely game.

-Unknown

-We Are All A Beautiful Mess-

12. Hidden

DEPRESSION PLAYED A MASSIVE PART IN PRODUCING my gritty and grainy monochrome captures with plenty of blacks and whites, greys and browns. Using earthy tones to represent the organic subject matter and the organic material all around. It was kind of like being at one with the dirt as it were, the dirt being my struggle, while my curves, lines and imperfections became the geography, the mapping of this ever-changing landscape that just so happened to be my body. All these elements joined together and became a favourite style of mine. I would go on to use it a lot in my photos because I found it visually and descriptively fitting.

You see, working in colour is a strange one for me. For a long time I felt colour did not really contribute to me telling my story, especially on those dark and depressive days, and although I did make a point of experimenting with it, each time I did made me question why as it just never seemed to feel right. After trying and being unsuccessful so many times in finding a process that worked for me, I started to wonder if perhaps it was a possibility that I had allowed outside influences to set off another cycle of the dreaded self-doubt.

I decided if that was indeed the case to not feel it was necessarily a bad thing, because it had rather the opposite effect: it actually strengthened my belief in regards to the artwork I was already creating, where I was already going, making me feel more positive in my creative decisions. This especially helped me when it came to my mood, and as unpredictable as it could be, no matter what stage of mood I was in it taught me to own my creativity and my vision. If I did decide to use colour in my artwork I realised that I needed to experiment with muted colours more. This actually brought me to a personal compromise from my frustrations about the use of colour, and I soon learned from asking myself lots of questions and being honest with the answers. I found new ways of portraying my mood and showing character. Let me tell you, with bipolar that is not always an easy thing to achieve.

You see, a lot of the time I only felt like using colour if I were possibly in one of my short hypomanic states, and even then I felt my personality and mood would still have been likened more to monochrome but perhaps with some accents of colour used at these times instead. Those accents of colour tended to be shades of blue, silver and green.

I decided to help myself a little and went on to do more research in colour theory to assist with my choices if and when I decided to try to add them to my works. This allowed me to express my personality and therefore maintain the honesty and vulnerability within my portraits which were so important to me, that I had worked hard to build up and was continually striving to maintain. Funnily enough this got me learning more about colour psychology, including more in-depth learning about the four colour personalities. It also led to me doing more research into personality, including tests associated with personality types such as 'Myers–Briggs' alongside the four temperaments: sanguine; phlegmatic; choleric; and melancholic.

Depression was a massive contributing factor, but there were also other factors for my low mood. I can tell you now that without a doubt, dealing with physical pain on a daily basis is one of the most dominant features resulting in the feeling of never being able to free yourself or break away from it. In my experience my MD has always been painful, so much so it dramatically reduced my quality of life. I found it to be a constant source of frustration and I knew it was a fundamental factor to any unwanted switch in my mood. Experiencing chronic pain was always going to be the hard part. So relentless in nature, so difficult to explain and therefore even harder to manage because it made you feel alienated and alone. Generalised muscle aches, topped up with the sensation of ripped muscles and tears. With a serving of shooting painful nerves running alongside a lactic acid burn. On top of bones that feel like you have been kicked by a horse, with whole mornings spent rigid and stiff, unable to move.

Constant fights against gravity with ligament tightness, contractures and more. Complimented by the gift of a constant cycle of fatigue, so overwhelming it stopped you in your tracks. All the while knowing this was pushing you further away from being able to hold your own. My brother and I have frequently said that for us, becoming pain free would be like waving goodbye to a devastating burden. That we would consider ourselves able to manage like "everyone else" if only we didn't experience these horrendous levels of disability, all due to pain. We have said to one another that we don't actually see the disease as such an emotional toll or see our physical issues so much of a burden, even though losing physical abilities like using our legs to walk or using our arms to lift is, of course, a life-changing thing. But physically having to stop doing things due to having a neuromuscular condition wouldn't be so tough if we could be given the chance of a pain-free existence. We know we could adapt, cope better, live happier lives and manage our muscular dystrophy symptoms better if this was indeed the case.

The evil we experience is the constant weight of a heavy, suffocating, overbearing blanket we call pain. That waits in the shadows to remind us of all that is to come and all the things we can no longer do. To make us feel worse, to tell us we aren't moving, stopping us from living a fuller life. Pain certainly can shut you off from the world and makes you feel like hiding away.

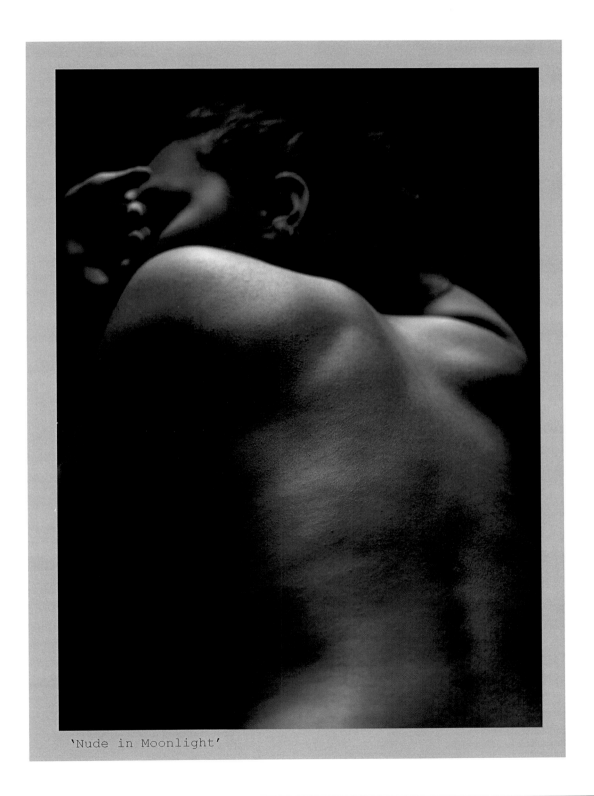

'Nude in Moonlight'

Hidden

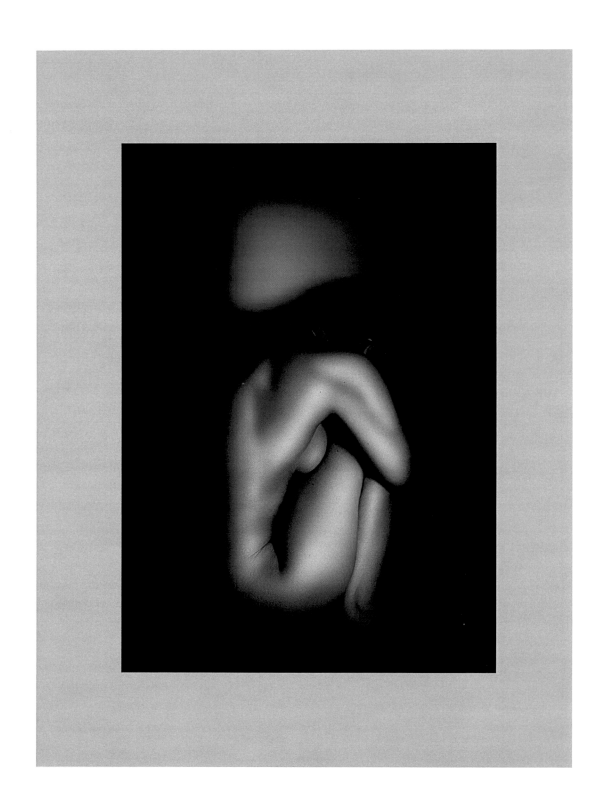

-We Are All A Beautiful Mess-

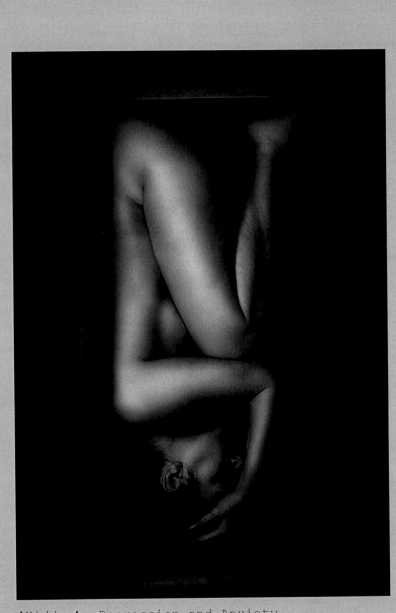

'Hidden' - Depression and Anxiety

Hidden

Hidden

She was hidden from the world,
in a cupboard in her mind.
Opening up the door,
someone special will only find.
The way to talk her out of,
the darkness she had become.
She was hidden from the world,
in a cupboard in her mind.

-We Are All A Beautiful Mess-

'Untitled'

Hidden

Someone I loved once gave me a box full of darkness.

It took me years to understand that this too, was a gift.

- Mary Oliver

'The Uses of Sorrow'

13. The Butterfly

I FOUND TAKING PHOTOGRAPHS EXTREMELY HEALING and a welcome distraction from feeling the effects of my disease. Of course, I felt physical pain when making artwork but it gave me focus, and at this point I was taking self-portraits and creating art more than ever before. I was confident in the direction of the creative path I was taking.

Actually, speaking of direction, not only did I realise my art was responsible for showing me the possibilities and opportunities that life still had to offer, it also made me realise that I was starting to cope much better with a disease that was so damn unpredictable. Not only that, I had been subconsciously able to address an accumulation of internal struggles that I had been battling with for many years. I realised that my creativity was now addressing these periods of past trauma, periods of my life that really took a hold of me and that subsequently haunted me. By continuing to take self-portraits and making art I became more aware that in the process I had not only been able to help other people but I recognised that I had been able to help myself to heal from this painful past.

The trauma had had a negative impact on every part of me for sure, but as much as that was true the power of creativity had such strength it paved the way for me to discover that life still had beauty after so many periods of heartbreak.

What I was experiencing was trauma-related growth, something I never thought was possible for someone like me and yet here I was, already feeling it and already growing from it. It took a lot of time, effort and one hell of a struggle, but ultimately I was left rewarded and reaping the psychological benefits of coming to terms with those dark days.

I was starting to enjoy a better human connection and I felt happier from experiencing a deeper appreciation for my own life. It also led to an understanding that this kind of growth could also be responsible for some people finding their religious faith, something I had heard a lot about but never actually understood. I personally have never been religious, and I don't think I ever will be, but after this period I realised I am spiritual in my own way.

I now understand when someone proclaims they have found god. My faith wasn't in god, but that didn't mean I wasn't experiencing a higher level of faith when it came to my life. Faith in my journey, faith in my story and faith in myself as a human being, and because of all of these things I was, in my opinion, becoming a better person from within. Someone I now look at and like for the very first time.

I always thought that I was incapable of this kind of growth. Due to my misconceptions and naivety I thought that growth in this way, on this level, was never going to be a reality for me. I never considered it a possibility. I was under the illusion that growth only happened for the resilient ones. It was my mistake in thinking that only people who are weak experience struggles while the strong experience growth, when on reflection I realised a possibility that those who already had more coping skills to start with maybe didn't experience this growth in such a profound way. I lost count of the amount of times art had picked me up from the floor. Given me a voice when sound would not come out and when I struggled to communicate any other way.

It helped me to attend my own art therapy sessions when the waiting lists were full. Put a smile back on my face when I felt down because I thought I had no skill. Raised my belief that I could indeed still achieve, even though I was doing something completely different to what I had originally set out to do. I started to understand the power of art, the power of photography and the huge place it had in my heart, in my life and the place it had in society.

Art contributed heavily towards an endless cycle of growth. It made sense of my truth, no matter how painful. It took that pain and made it into something beautiful. Still, even with this profound growth within me, thanks to my illnesses I never always knew where I was going in my life, but photography and art helped me find some peace in that.

My direction was changing daily and there was nothing I could do about it. It was all part of having a progressive disease and I just had to learn to ride those waves a little better, veer around those winding paths with a little confidence and navigate using art to help me find the beauty in mystery and remembering to put trust in my destiny, even with a chronic illness, pain and disease.

My journey and navigation through life is no doubt what helped me to find my own artistic style, and of course it is a style that no one can truly replicate, not fully, not really, for it only comes from my unique personality, my mind, my road trip in life, my dreams, my aspirations. My own personal style is living and breathing, and as it continues to evolve my personal accents and traits run through my artwork like the blood runs through my veins. It is my own artistic fingerprint.

Creativity will always come from within me and I have learned it is not to be feared. I will no longer suppress it for fear of being misunderstood. I will keep speaking my truth in my way and I will keep taking photographs and capturing emotion all the time it makes sense for me to do so because all the time it gives me something valuable that nothing else can, I know I am always going to be doing it right.

Telling my own story, I have realised, is important where once I thought it was just self-indulgent and vain. I soon understood that my low self-esteem and fear of rejection was rearing its ugly head when I felt those things. So I just kept asking myself the question: how can that be if it gives someone else hope?

Now hope is what I expressed right at the beginning, that it was a necessary and powerful thing, because hope is what gave me the belief that I would keep going. It gave me the freedom to explore, the freedom to conquer my fears, even when life was so damn hard, and it gave me the ability and the tools to reach within myself and believe there would be better days ahead.

Butterfly Series - Survival of Trauma - 'Attraction'

The Butterfly

Butterfly Series - 'Faith'

-We Are All A Beautiful Mess-

Butterfly Series - 'Closure'

The Butterfly

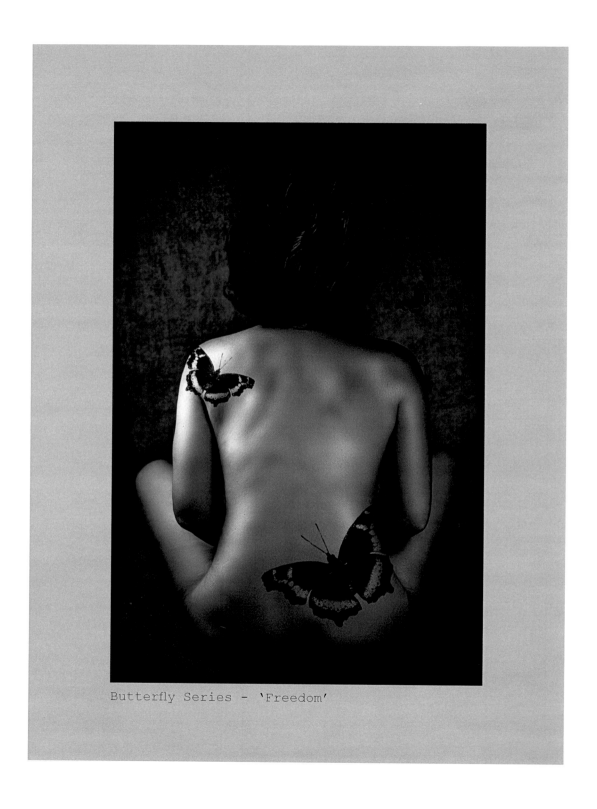

Butterfly Series - 'Freedom'

-We Are All A Beautiful Mess-

Butterfly Series - 'Butterfly Kiss'

The Butterfly

The creative adult is the child who survived.

-Ursula K. Le Guin

-We Are All A Beautiful Mess-

14. The Child on the Stairs

LIFE IS FULL OF SUPRISES. SOME SUPRISES ARE BETTER than others, and beginning any new journey because of life's situations forcing its hand is definitely one of those surprises.

Well, in my case, it felt as if life was dragging me through the mud, taking me in the complete opposite direction to where I wanted to go and, of course, I was busy digging my heels into the ground. Causing damage and destruction at every proverbial mile reached.

When I was young, I was always the more stubborn of the siblings. By stubborn, I mean screaming. Sat screaming at every single step I sat on the staircase on the way up to my bedroom where I had been sent to 'do my time' for being naughty for one thing or another, making a scene every single step of the way, which of course made the whole punishment and 'time out' last so much longer for me. My brother, on the other hand, had it figured out: go quietly, do your time and get out early for good behaviour, and I see of course, that this was the smarter option, but it was the option I couldn't see at the time. I was too blinded by my own descending 'red mist'.

Some would have said I was the epitome of a hot-headed Scorpio child with a slight sting in her tail and an even bigger chip on her shoulder. I would cross my arms and battle right until the bitter end, the bitter end being mostly a product of wasted time of protest from me as it always ended in defeat. Having time added to my 'sentence' and most likely landing me in my room for the rest of the evening with nothing much to show for it, except a possible sore throat for my efforts, and all made worse by the fact I would be missing out on some much needed apple crumble and ice cream by night time.

I found it difficult to keep a lid on my emotions growing up because I would often find it hard to describe how I was feeling. I found it even harder to understand why I was feeling the range of emotions I experienced, and it often made me feel quite inadequate and weak, which resulted in protest a lot of the time.

However, years later and here I am, a full-fledged adult coping with all different types of situations and difficulties associated with a life of chronic illness. The more I went through in relation to my muscular dystrophy and secondary conditions, the more I learned I would achieve more if I stopped dragging my heels in protest.

I learned that I could actually take those traits and elements of my character and turn them into an integral resource that I could use to fight with instead. I would use them to not give up on myself as I continued to not only make my way through life but make a life for myself while coping better at navigating the medical mine-field. As my muscular dystrophy progressed my ability to move got harder. Muscles continued to get weaker, stiffer, and I continued to tire easily from the smallest of tasks. It was all very difficult to deal with.

But the hardest issue I had faced at that point on top of everything else were the ongoing symptoms of my gastrointestinal disorder. Since my oesophageal muscles weakened my stomach stopped working, and as my stomach stopped working my bowel became sluggish and unable to function correctly which left me in a rather frustrating, desperate and heartbreaking situation. The whole process was mind-boggling and so very tiring. Trying different liquid enteral feeds, different types of nutritional supplements, dealing with an inactive bowel and all that comes with that.

Sickness, bloating, urine and stoma infections and lots of medications which led to new side effects from those medications and then me being prescribed medications to combat the unwanted side effects, leaving me with, you guessed it, more side effects. It really was a toss-up between the lesser of many evils. Then there was the constant monitoring, the hospital admissions, dietician appointments, gastro consultations, enteral feeding nurse visits and constant head-scratching due to recurrent infections and ongoing pain. It really was so time consuming. It was always uncomfortable and it just left me feeling out of control of being able to care for myself. I felt lost and it made my head hurt, the blood pumping between my ears, leaving me feeling dizzy and in a spin. I found myself desperate for a better quality of life.

In all of the challenging times I had faced so far, this was quite possibly one of the worst and I really felt I had lost all control. But that being said, during the worst times it seemed just when I felt I had no fight left to give, I would surprise myself as I started to roll my sleeves up. This was the time I actually found myself thanking that little girl, the one that used to sit on the stairs with her arms folded, declaring war. Because you know what? She had actually given me something valuable, something of use in my adult life. And even though I struggled so much with all my medical care, my needs and my long list of complex diagnoses, out of all the things about me I thought I had lost through illness alone, I realised the one thing I clearly hadn't lost or given up for anyone or anything was my stubbornness.

I know that stubbornness in general can sometimes be a difficult trait and it hasn't always sat comfortably with me, but in this situation and in my life as it is now, I am so grateful for the little girl still hanging on in there, red-faced and steaming from the ears, spitting feathers and being my strength.

This strength is what got me through the next phase of my disease progression and it allowed me to open my eyes a little more. I could see more clearly the journey I had been on to get to this point. How I had grown as an individual to even accept this next challenge, let alone to face it head on. Having a gastrostomy feeding tube fitted had such a profound effect on me in every single way. Having to have one so damn quickly had scared me so much, that in the end it actually made me want to live more.

It made me live in the moment and work on not being too scared of the future, which I am always going to be working on. It enabled me to experience new things, to plan and do things I have always wanted to do regardless of my disposition in life with my anxiety, depression, bipolar and physical disabilities, and let me tell you, for me to even feel this way and experience the positives of wanting to do these things, even that in itself was a massive change for me. A huge achievement in such adverse circumstances.

To be honest, having a lifelong, intense condition had made me feel numb; I guess it was a coping mechanism – better to not feel anything at all – but I just didn't want to feel numb anymore. So once again I thanked the child for her folded arms, refusing to give up, and even though I found it to be a scary existence a lot of the time I thanked modern medicine for keeping me alive.

As I felt all these feelings and dealt with all the heightened emotions, I managed to make a decision. I decided to not just make art by taking pictures but to take the feeling I got from creating art and use that feeling to find the beauty in everything, especially in difficult moments. Choosing to keep breathing and to experience new things. To travel to new places and take in every moment, to not dwell on the past. To live. So with that mindset I did just that, and while I learned to start concentrating on living a more fulfilling life, I continued taking photos and making new self-portrait art.

I photographed every line, bump, lump, stretch mark and surgery scar that I once hated the sight of and would once apon a time never show. I photographed my feeding tube, my wasting legs, my winging scapula and just about all of my insecurities. I photographed myself on my better days, my good days and on my OK days. On bad days and kept documenting just after my worst days. I documented my life in the moment, raw and authentic, and I felt so alive! I used this documentation to raise awareness of conditions, to raise awareness of mental health illnesses and to raise awareness of body confidence issues that affect so many people in every walk of life.

I wanted to send a message in the hope that it would successfully reach people, people like me in similar situations, or any situation that required inner strength from an uphill struggle, who perhaps would benefit greatly from someone sharing their innermost feelings, insecurities, and vulnerabilities, turning full circle to tell a positive story and to send out a positive message of the importance of hope.

I was, of course, proud when my work reached organisations with a similar focus and caught the attention of artists. But it has to be said, it was nothing compared to those messages of support I received from someone who was going through their version of hell, expressing their gratitude by letting me know that my artwork and words had reached them and most importantly that it had made a positive difference to their day. If only we could bottle that feeling.

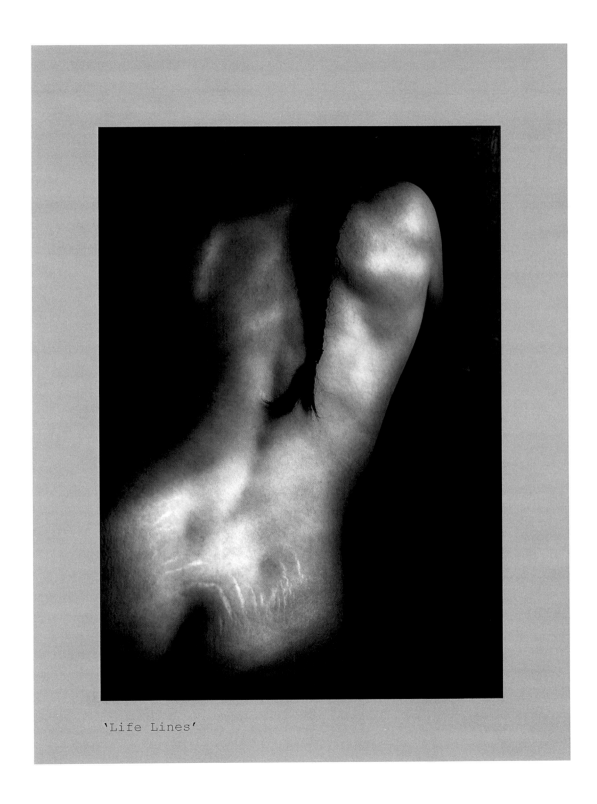

'Life Lines'

'Metamorphic' - The scientific process involving
mutations, growth and change.

-We Are All A Beautiful Mess-

The Child on the Stairs

Art is my cure to all this madness, sadness and loss of

belonging in the world and through it

I'll walk myself home.

-Nikki Rowe

-We Are All A Beautiful Mess-

15. Coming Home

AN ART COLLECTOR IN CHELSEA, LONDON NOW OWNS 'Alternative Sadness' one of my favourite pieces from my nude self-portrait collection. She said once she had seen it, she just knew she could never part with it. It was such a beautiful and fulfilling experience for me.

Not only does this lovely lady have one of my favourite pieces of artwork to date, but she also has the biggest photograph from my self-portrait series on display within her home.

A graphic designer for Qantas airlines living in Victoria, Australia owns a special edition piece from the 'The Hobbit' series which he hand-framed and hung in his apartment overlooking the city.

Two separate collectors in Italy now own a limited edition piece from a series called 'Hidden' and another from a limited edition called 'Dreams'.

A collector in Paris, France and two separate art collectors in different parts of America all have limited edition prints of 'Dreams'.

You can imagine it made me feel quite amazing, and as lovely as it all was to have my work appreciated in this way it still won't ever compare to how I felt when I received a message from a man called Lee, who wanted to own framed prints from one of my early phone series.

He decided he would also like the words from my Instagram post to be added in with the framed images. He said the words really resonated with him. I was only too happy to accommodate his wishes, and after we had spent time messaging backwards and forwards talking about framing options, paper and font types for the text, he said thank you and told me to keep fighting the good fight. It turns out he also had limb-girdle muscular dystrophy type 2a.

I spent time working on myself because producing art helped me to see what I needed to improve on. Some people might look at a photo of themselves and think, *I want to improve on my body so I will go to the gym.* But that wasn't really an option for me, so in that sense I just had to accept me for me and work on making sure I looked after myself emotionally as much as I could.

Over the course of my teenage and adult life I had had four major breakdowns. There were times in my life where I was so delicate and easily damaged, I really never ever thought I would repair, I thought I would be stuck in the darkness forever more. Always wondering what it would be like to be someone else instead, I didn't even see becoming a better version of myself as even an option for me.

But this was all down to my mental health problems and low self-esteem. Being around the wrong people at impressionable ages and making desperate decisions alone, when at those times I could have done with some support and much needed guidance. You see, what I have learned since being more open and honest with myself is this: if you stop and think too much about what your disease may be doing to you, then you are just spending all your time being mentally paralysed by the fear before your disease has taken hold of you in a physical sense.

Being stopped or slowed by progression is going to happen at some point in the future, so why should I let this fear stop me now? All it is doing is robbing me of all my life in the here and now, the present, this moment. Tomorrow is not here yet, but I am here now. At what point am I going to stop procrastinating and let it all out?

I could still set personal goals and objectives and I had to remind myself that no two people's ideas of personal achievements are ever going to be the same. I had spent too many years being so damn hard on myself, and for what? It only gave me more fear. I cannot forget why I do what I do. I cannot forget the fundamentals. The reason, the purpose, the destination. I cannot do myself the injustice of falling back into the trap, the one where I was good enough, but my brain constantly told me otherwise. I used to get so frustrated and disheartened when my creativity stopped and I ended up in a funk of the dreaded creative block.

My bipolar made me feel like I had to not only reach the finish line but cross it triumphantly or else it was a failure. I never measured it by whether I was emotionally ready or not. I now live in the moment and take my time; after all, don't the good things come to those who wait? Creative projects end, but only temporarily. It is to help you to stop and rest for a while, in preparation for embarking on something great! I have learned not to get so downbeat about my lack of mobility, because my lack of mobility does not measure my other abilities or strengths, and that is another reason why I am unique. I have learned that no one in the world can be me and that means I am already achieving. By truly accepting who I am I follow my heart, and while I am still finding my way I am so pleased I took that step, because if I hadn't have had that courage I would have never have satisfied my soul. If I didn't take the good from the bad situations, I wouldn't have been able to make them into art. I wouldn't have become an artist.

For me, creativity means the presence of passion, and I am an extremely passionate person. I have always been. Passion is what makes me feel alive. Creativity forces me out of the darkness and pushes me in front of myself to make me visualise and therefore remember all the beauty in my life and not to forget the beauty all around. It helps me to harvest it from within. It allows me to realise that my voice is just as important as anyone else's and for the first time in my life I realise I have always had something worthwhile to say. I have a voice and people who like my words, like my works. And those who like my work appreciate the stories within them, this is something that is not to be given up on!

Making art and taking photographs is something to show that are real and tangible parts of my life. It is my being. It shows my resilience and my character that has evolved from that painful seed of self-destruction and self-doubt that has cracked, grown in strength, and taken on the world. It will be the evidence of my being that will go on forever and that won't ever fade or die. Creativity has allowed me to explore who I really am. It has created a freedom nothing else has been able to give me in this way.

It has allowed me to navigate within myself until I have found real happiness, even when I have and will always struggle with maintaining my mental health. Creativity allows me to keep opening those doors and to remind myself that I am not to be constrained and that I am so much more than my disease, illnesses and conditions. I am a multidimensional being capable of continuous growth, and my possibilities are endless. Taking photographs and making art from them is in turn creating a beautiful catalogue of hopeful moments to store. Documenting the making of a brand-new mindset and seeing that I have a valuable life. It has given me the tools to explain so eloquently how I feel and I never have to be stumped trying to find a single one of those eloquent words. I am an introverted being, and even though I create my art in solitude I am so happy to know it will bring people together. It has allowed me to start powerful discussions, has given me new friendships, allowed me to meet like-minded people and found me more MD family members than I could only ever imagine I would meet!

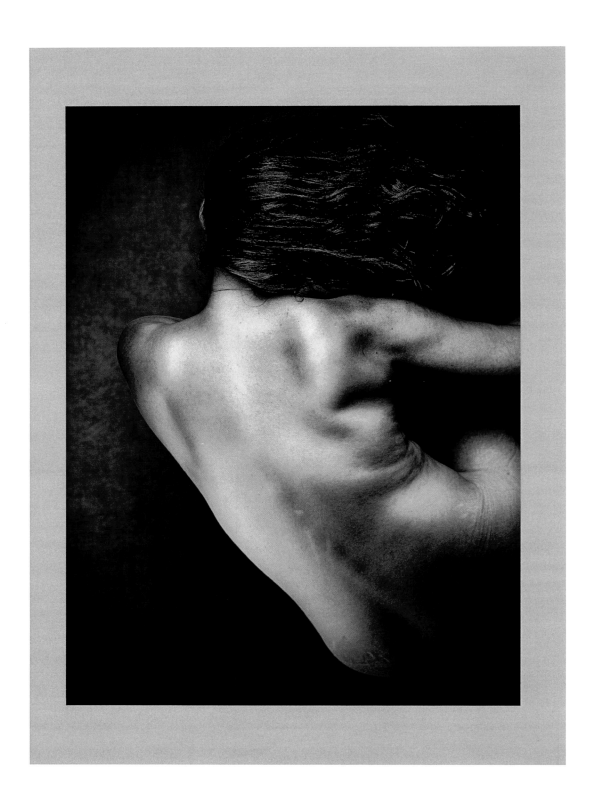

-We Are All A Beautiful Mess-

'Internal Struggle'

Making a difference to other people and knowing my artwork is reaching them, is one of the most rewarding
elements of creativity....

Hi Gems!

*I found your page through friends who both have been a great
support to me since finding out our daughter Jessica has LGMD 2D
(she just turned 10).*

*I'd just like to say looking through your posts with Jessica we both
feel you're a huge inspiration to her and just finding you at the right
time, as now it's sunk into Jess she is having a few days of "why me?"
But seeing your posts have shown her it doesn't have to take control
of who you are. Jess has decided she wants to become a vet and started studying some veterinarian anatomy books as she loves to read
and learn new things. She has made it her mission too, to help fund
and find a cure so is always busy fundraising. We just this week managed to get quite a few companies to sign up for the Go Orange Day!
Hopefully one day we will find a cure.*

We look forward to hearing from you and hope you are well.

Much love, Kelly & Jessica xx

As a lady with MD I am excited for you to be publishing your experiences.
You do amazing things with all your passions.
You are incredibly gifted – and an artist in every way – and just so incredibly special. The world needs to hear what you have to share. I absolutely cannot wait. The parts that accompany your art move me so profoundly so it's time others who need your strength receive it.

****

I look forward to seeing more of your artistic work and reading more of your stories, many people in this world often view disabled people differently and you have demonstrated in such a beautiful and artistic way that there is such depth and beauty in each and every single one of us, disabled or not.
Keep up the great work, sending you positive vibes and much love from Australia.

****

I love your self-portraits, they are very beautiful and I can relate to how this is healing. I have myotonic muscular dystrophy. I feel like I am only a fraction of what I used to be 10 years ago. I try not to focus on that and I try to be so grateful for my present life and hope for the future.
I wish you well!

'The Hobbit'

-We Are All A Beautiful Mess-

16. Dare to Dream

NEW-FOUND FRIENDS FILLED MY DAYS WITH POSITIVE THOUGHTS. More stories of hope, resistance, strength and laughter reached me and reached me exactly when I needed it.

Bad days were still to be had, but the heavy load you carry on your shoulders created by chronic illness was never quite as heavy when the weight was being shared between friends. My camera batteries always needed charging, as did my power chair (and myself!).

As each day passed new creative ideas bubbled up and out of me like a volcano, thick and fast and so much so I had to start making a list to get the ideas down on paper, I didn't want to risk losing those ideas. It annoyed me somewhat to have to do this, because I prefer my art to be born from pure spontaneity, and I still very much like the idea of not really planning my photos at all – I preferred to just set up and see where the mood would take me. But with different ideas forming so fast and coupled with the muscular dystrophy progressing too, I found that I couldn't ignore or hide my need to rest a lot more, and I found myself having to take longer pauses in between creating. This became a gradual thing, something I had been quietly noting and trying to ignore for quite some time. It started at first only being a few days of rest in-between shooting for the sake of general recovery, then that recovery time frame increased to a little over a week depending on how much physical exertion and movement the shoot consisted of. This time frame went on to increase further, way beyond that initial period. My body was slowing down a little more each time and it ached and hurt and sometimes just screamed at me to stop. I would then find the break between photos being one or even two months apart.

This was unsettling and upsetting and I felt at times I would have to give it up, so at these times I was grateful for the list of ideas. They came in handy as they served as a mental note to myself when I started to struggle that I wasn't finished yet, and it also enabled me to keep creatively busy by being able to feel I could get ideas and add to my story even while I recovered and spent months at a time in bed. In the end I gave up heavy duty photography and the use of certain setups. Flash lights and softboxes and light stands were cast aside and I ended up with the most basic kit.

I worked more and more with natural light and the available sources and make-shift setups all around. It helped to ease the frustration of failed works using heavy duty stands, and minimised smashed kit as a result of tired arms and a weakened body. I pretty much resigned myself to accepting the fact I physically didn't have the strength to keep setting stuff up anymore, so I went to having just the camera and tripod nearby at all times. This made it far easier to grab and get going when-ever I felt the creative urge calling.

I was never a trained photographer, or a schooled artist for that matter. Due to illness I was taken out of my comfort zone and worked on teaching myself photography. Technical skills are still needed, of course, and have to be understood and applied for sure. But for me it is and always has been a feeling – taking photos is purely driven by emotion and soul, and it is an emotion which keeps the honesty within my photography alive.

I'm not unorthodox on purpose, I just create how I create because it is the only way I know how. I photograph in the moment, technically correct or not. If I like it, I like it – I don't care too much about the rules. It's the same with framing – I frame things as I see them and for me, if I think too much about the technicalities I miss the impact and identification and the reason for the capture. I could have missed out on the shot of all shots and to me, that would just be a crime.

Everything outside of being a mum to two self-sufficient teens was pretty much about creating, and I was extremely lucky that they were so supportive of my projects and understood fully the reasons behind them. They knew that it was a positive move and a highly therapeutic release for me. I must say, I was extremely proud of them for the way they handled it. I mean, their mum taking naked photos to create art? Doesn't it just sound like a topic of utter embarrassment for anyone's offspring, at any age, let alone the embarrassment levels of said teenagers when it comes to the topic of nude art? But they surprised me, it was like they already knew the benefits I reaped from creating and in return they got to experience the benefits, too – a happier, healthier and calmer mum to name a few.

These guys had seen me at my worst. They saw me fighting anxiety and depression prior to my diagnosis of muscular dystrophy, then they witnessed the fallout from that. They witnessed my good days and bad days, they witnessed it all and still they never ever judged me for any of my issues, they never did, not ever, not once. I will always remember having a chat with them both about how they felt about my photographic projects, and of course the subject of what I photographed had to be spoken about. When I possibly wanted to start posting some of my works online, it was an especially important discussion.

I was fully expecting a protest of epic proportions and I would have completely understood. I had already said to myself prior to our conversation that if they hated the very thought of it, I wouldn't publicly share anything. My kids' happiness is always going to come first.

As it turned out I needn't have worried, as they both shocked me when they said "Why wouldn't you, mum? We understand why you do this, we understand this is art!" You see, as a family the benefits and positive outcomes outweighed any potential negatives, and even when it came to doing the medical care and monotonous tasks associated with my illness I felt that I was able to cope better with these tasks in general, and I felt my anxiety had reduced since being able to have this steady artistic focus in my life.

The practical things that were once really difficult for me (and everyone else for that matter), such as managing emotionally, I was now finding more manageable, simply because I would be able to take myself off within my mind for a while when needed. And while successfully completing the medical tasks - which I ended up resenting - were such a time-consuming part of my day, I'd spend the time daydreaming about my next project. I would also use this time to make sure I kept my friendships going by replying to messages, especially from people like my MD friends. Friends who understood most of my challenges, would never judge me, and would spur me on as I would them. I would also spend these times chatting about all things arty, with like-minded people that I had also struck up great friendships with along the way.

My immediate family were initially taken aback by my projects, but that was only because they were nude shots. They had of course never seen me in this way, and some found it hard to see previously hidden evidence of disease. They still showed their support, and over time became familiar with the direction of my photography. They even ended up having their own favourite pieces, which actually led me to make a decision to start printing my works and to introduce the whole process of printing, signing and framing original and limited edition pieces. These then became gifts for each of those family members that had expressed their love for a certain photograph and appreciated the story behind it. Come what may with my disease, it was a good feeling to know that I was actively leaving a legacy, and that pieces of artwork and my story were being hung up in my family's homes.

I am lucky as I come from a very creative family, and most of my family can paint and draw using many mediums. They have a love for photography and have a great eye for detail when it comes to creating.

My grandmother on my mum's side painted scenes of the little village she lived in, using oil and watercolour. I always remember being completely drawn into her paintings whenever I visited as a child.

My mum was a talented pastel artist who could draw from memory and reference. She created beautiful wildlife scenes with pastel on paper, but her self-portrait hanging up in her living room will always be my favourite for sure. Aunties and cousins on both sides could draw, photograph, craft and sew, and uncles could build and construct out of near enough anything.

My dad and brother honed their craft by being musically minded, extremely talented in composing music, playing instruments and song writing. They were both able to pick up and play just about any instrument they set their sights on, successfully composing, creating music, songwriting and recording. When I was growing up, some of my favourite memories were hearing my dad and my brother play guitar together, and my dad and his dad (my granddad) playing the sax together, those moments now I am older I appreciate so much; once you have heard and felt those beautiful rich sounds they truly are unforgettable.

'Summoning of Strength'

-We Are All A Beautiful Mess-

'The Last Dance'

Dare to Dream

A photograph is a secret about a secret.

The more it tells you the less you know.

— Diane Arbus

17. The Hyacinth Bulb

I FOUND MYSELF NATURALLY CREATING SERIES AFTER SERIES, and each one spoke those words out loud. Those words that were notoriously hard to form, those words that never flowed, never just rolled off the tongue. They would hardly ever reach the tongue, and if they did? They would be uncomfortable and challenging to hold there in the mouth, heavy like a ball bearing. They would just roll backwards like in a pinball machine and become lodged in my throat, causing a stress lump of all things. Those damn words. Those words that made me feel like I was the only one. Those words I truly didn't want to sound out.

They always gave me a fear of speaking; I always had a fear of being misunderstood. At other times I could, depending on my mood, find myself creating a series of images that didn't seem to make any sense to me whatsoever when pressing the shutter, or those photos that I thought were missing a vital piece of the puzzle, photos that I had cast aside unable to figure out why I had taken them, only to find that months later they had me jigging up and down in my chair and smiling with joy as the pieces came together and told the story of that moment, proving I had taken them extremely well.

If I could have kicked myself I would have, and sometimes I would just sit and curse; other times I would just sit with my mouth open feeling like I'd had that eureka moment – the light went on and there it was. I realised I was reaching a point in my photography where, through my storytelling, I was addressing key topics.

To me it was always going to be a personal projection, but people were also reaching out and familiarising with those personal projections too.

I never thought that it could happen, but my photographs and the stories behind them seemed to address topics that affected many, topics that were also the words that other people got stuck in their throats and which were hard for them to talk about. Topics that were at risk of being poorly understood and therefore resulted in people feeling alone. I realised that with my photography, I was not only speaking my truth about my own personal life but I was, through creativity, encouraging others to speak their truth too. This was important. I realised this was no longer just about my survival dealing with a muscle-wasting disease, it was so much more than that.

This was not only addressing my disease progression but it was addressing mental health, creative therapy and the importance of communicating and bringing people together. Letting people who perhaps felt lonely know that they didn't have to be alone, that within creative minds they had friends riding the storm; that when they needed support, they had some place familiar to go. Showing there is still hope to be felt even when you feel hopeless, bright light to be seen after the darkness and to no longer fear those dark days as it was all part of the process and necessary for positive change to occur.

It got me thinking back to when I was a child in first school, in the little village where I grew up. The school was very small and only had two classrooms. There was an outbuilding that housed a row of old outside toilets from back in the day, and although we didn't use it for its original purpose (I, for one, was extremely grateful for that), the building did serve another, more creative purpose. Each winter all the children would get a cardboard pot from the teacher, which we would decorate with materials out of the arts and craft tray, materials like silver papers, foils, pompoms and pipe cleaners which we got to colour with crayons and felt tip pens and make tissue paper flowers and trees, and we'd glaze our creations with lashings of PVA glue to finish.

We would then fill our pots with compost and we each got our very own hyacinth bulb to plant. When we had finished we would take our pots to the old outside toilets and hide the hyacinth bulbs away in the darkness for the winter months. In the long, bleak, dark and cold season, it gave us something to look forward to after the celebrations of Christmas had all passed.

When the springtime came, we would eagerly venture out to collect our pots to find the bulbs had sprouted and the stems had formed, peeking inside the shoot where a touch of colour could be seen starting to appear. It was a time that was so full of excitement and pure happiness, and this memory has served as a reminder throughout my whole life that to experience the glory of life we still need to push through the darkness to be able to reach full bloom.

'Apologies'

-We Are All A Beautiful Mess-

'The Evolution of Hope'

The Hyacinth Bulb

-We Are All A Beautiful Mess-

'Bipolar Dawn' Part 2

There will always be those who look only at technique, who ask 'how' while other of a more curious nature will ask 'why'. Personally, I have always preferred inspiration to information.

– Man Ray

-We Are All A Beautiful Mess-

18. The Cello

SOMETIMES I THINK LIFE CAN BE VERY MUCH LIKE LEARNING to play the cello, with an unskilled hand holding the bow. It can make you grit your teeth, make you want to hold your hands over your ears at the same time as wanting to run for the hills, never to return!

With its high-pitched scratching noises piercing your ear drums, its tuning pegs constantly slipping out of place, seemingly on every single turn you make. It can become a noise tormenting the auditory-sensitive, a noise that feels like it has the power to potentially destroy your soul. You just want and need it to stop. It can become overwhelming and chaotic, and even when trying so hard it can still feel like you are being screamed at because you are just not doing it right.

The thing is, with life is there is no definitive way of 'doing it right'. Now I am no expert; I speak from my own personal experiences, and I feel that it is important to point that out. But what I have personally found is that you can't afford to put that bow down. If you do that is OK, but you must pick it back up again. You have to keep going, you have to keep practicing and playing those strings over and over, because if you give up on the cello you give up on yourself, and then you give up on life. Give up on life, and there is nowhere else to go.

Living with bipolar disorder, battling anxiety and depression to then to be diagnosed with a muscle-wasting condition on top of all that, I think it would be fair to say that when I have struggled with the symptoms of these conditions the truth and reality is that giving up on life crossed my mind on many occasions. On each of those occasions it was a very real and scary ride. And even though I have experienced such feelings and thoughts, I consider myself extremely lucky. Although these moments and thought processes have been extremely troublesome when they are present, and I sometimes find myself worrying about if they should return, they have thankfully been fleeting moments in time. Fleeting enough for me to get a handle on the situation, fleeting enough to pull myself through them, and of paramount importance has been having the right support and help when I have been scared of feeling misunderstood and so alone in my mind.

Ultimately I am thankful I have always had the ability, when it matters most, to speak out and voice my fears to someone I know, someone I trust when these thoughts flash quickly through my mind. I can instantly recognise them, and through experience I know that if I want them out of my head, I soon find myself speaking the words even if it is a scared and whispered sound.

I am aware that for many people they have not been so lucky, and that truly makes me feel so incredibly sad because they perhaps just couldn't speak out loud those words that I can.

Playing that cello in life is difficult, and it is a fact that my situation has made it a massive pain in the arse. Having to cope with overlapping conditions has certainly made it feel like an extreme burden and at times like a completely impossible task, but with patience and time and lots of support it can actually be mastered. Playing the cello is my metaphor for life, and although it can be hard it can be achieved. You can still learn to play beautiful music.

It got me thinking more and more about how many people struggle to reach people for help. Especially the struggle to reach those who have the time and the patience - and in this fast-paced world? - to reach them in plenty of time. It got me thinking about how many of those people struggle to get a consistent amount of support when they need it the most.

This got me thinking about the wider benefits of my creative release and my own personal experiences and the benefits I had experienced so far in relation to my photography and self-portraits. My relationship with myself, my perception of myself, my body image, the way I was coping emotionally; the therapy that the whole experience gave me and the tools it provided me with to start making positive changes to my mindset, and in turn those positive moments, that progress, turned into positive actions moving forward. I had the opportunity to express myself when I needed to the most, and that was the defining point. To express myself when I needed to the most. In a beneficial way. In a way that helped me to pick up that bow after putting it down. Every single time.

'The Cello'- Life is hard, learn to play it well.

Thank you for the tragedy, I need it for my art.

-Kurt Cobain

-We Are All A Beautiful Mess-

19. Wabi-Sabi and Bathroom Tiles

THOSE CRACKED TILES IN THE BATHROOM, the ones I have mentioned once or twice before, had been hanging on quite willfully until I rather frustratingly knocked them off the wall accidentally with my wheelchair. Those tiles that ended up broken into pieces all over the floor.

Those tiles that have always caught my attention since that very first self-portrait, the one I took with my phone as I sat there curled up naked, early in the morning, totally oblivious to the journey I would now find myself on. I failed to see their importance at the time. It was those same tiles on that same day as I captured my mood that I made a very honest and personal confession to myself: that I indeed felt broken. I felt like a broken object with a broken life.

This was not just any kind of confession and this was not just any kind of broken – at this time I felt broken beyond all chance of repair. Those same tiles that my eyes got drawn to every single time I entered this room, and my eyes got drawn to each and every day thereafter. Those tiles served as a constant reminder to all those thoughts and feelings I had at the beginning. And as funny as it seems and as crazy as it sounds those tiles became a permanent feature in my mind, an important symbol reminding me to keep moving forward, that there are always choices in life, reminding me of those choices I made when I was at my lowest.

Those tiles reminded me that it is a fact of life that even the toughest of things break. They can break into only two or three pieces or they can break shattering into a million fragments. But either way, the amount of breakage doesn't matter, it doesn't matter whether it ends up being a few or many breaks – both objects deserve to be fixed in equal amounts. It was then that I realised their profound importance: those cracked tiles were actually me. You see, those tiles served as a reminder that I am the person who makes the decisions regarding my own mental and physical health. I am the one that has a choice in my life to replace or repair, and if I make that choice to repair I am responsible for helping myself have a better experience of life.

Those tiles got me thinking about Japanese aesthetics, in particular the concept of wabi-sabi, the idea that you can find beauty in impermanent and imperfect things, something that has always resonated with me.

Sometimes, however, my mental illness has gotten in the way, disturbing those good ideas and casting them aside. I was left feeling deeply tricked by the darkness in my mind. This led me to explore the ancient art of kintsugi, the idea that the broken object is never thrown away, it is instead fixed in an elaborate and artistic way. The object that is to be fixed is repaired in such a way that the cracks are turned into an eye-catching feature through the use of a super strong glue made with gold, so the imperfections can be seen and celebrated. A celebration of strength, a strength built from trauma and a deep beauty in the fact the object was once broken.

In kintsugi the process is a magnificent one and it is a perfect metaphor to apply to many areas of life, particularly for embracing and finding the often-hidden beauty in a person's own imperfections and flaws. But using kintsugi in your everyday life is something that takes a lot of patience, commitment and time, and even if you find you're not quite ready to open up to yourself a cracked bathroom tile is a good place to start. Kintsugi got me thinking about the pieces of my own story, the emotional journey I made after experiencing trauma, and the journey I am still on. I am sure for some people like me, the thought of being able to fix yourself doesn't ever ring true, and the signposts named "change" are overgrown with thorns and nettles which makes reading them extremely hard to do. I have had a lot of experience with trying to continually embrace my multitude of flaws. I really needed to reach for that gold-infused glue.

I had previously captured a self-portrait series which I had taken using my own interpretation of another concept in Japanese aesthetics, a concept known as yūgen, something I couldn't explain but have always felt, and it is funny because yūgen means exactly that. And even though yūgen can differ in meaning depending on the context, it can encompass the meaning of beauty in human sadness, and that really resonated with me. It rang true to my life and my situation, my melancholic art documenting my ongoing struggles and the sadness I had often strongly fought against along the way. Yūgen is not a physical process like kintsugi, rather a feeling that refers to an indescribable experience in life or the beauty in nature that is felt by the person in a profound and often very mysterious way. My relationship with my camera and my photographic art has many times had me experiencing these profound feelings, and has indeed enforced the relevance of yūgen as it has kintsugi in my everyday life.

The excitement to be able to experience complete freedom of expression even before I reach for that camera, every single time an idea starts to enter my mind, every single time I watch the light fill a room with wonder. Every time I see the shadows forming, every time I get into a brand-new pose, every time I challenge myself and my body to explore a new mindset, every time I get that magical feeling when every single idea is new. Every single time I wake up in the middle of the night to write a verse or a poem, every single time I express my truth.

All these things carry feelings you just cannot articulate or put into words, like the feeling you get as the night rolls in and you witness a clear sky of brightly lit stars. Every time the birds fly in perfect sequence heading towards the horizon chasing the clouds. Every time the wind howls through the trees and you feel your soul dancing with the swaying branches or the magic that is the burning red sky as you sit and watch the sun go down in the summer. That feeling that is more than pure euphoria, a feeling that you just can't quite put a word to or give a name no matter how much you try.

In my artwork I include the fact that life is not perfect and the idea that there is a beauty in that. Nothing lasts forever and nothing is ever finished. My photography will always make sure of that. The need to capture every moment and continue to document my art - my life - from those photographs, and to be safe in the knowledge that I am making a difference even if it is just to one other person, is now of importance. Because isn't that how, in the end, positive change comes about?

If one other person looks in the mirror and loves and appreciates what they see, when they look at the cracks that they have glued back together with a beautiful shimmer of golden strength and feel proud of themselves, if just one person accepts one fragment of who they truly are to start them on their journey, then in the end, loving themselves in all entirety won't feel like such a hard bloody task.

Being creative continues to teach me new things about myself every single time I use that creativity. It has already shown me in my darkest hour that I possessed the courage to fight a disease. When I thought I couldn't cope with chronic pain because I thought it would break me, and when a mental health condition had me riding those rolling waves of despair. And on those real bad days? Experience the want and desire to find the beauty within the sadness, the importance of the darkness, the journey in personal growth and the want and determination to make art from it and to love yourself with all you have, because to love yourself is a fundamental requirement to be able to survive whatever you are going through in life.

I will probably always find this a challenge, and I won't say I find it easy or that I will ever be completely fixed. After all, this will always be about my truth. But with art as my focus and my acceptance more forthcoming, I am starting to appreciate there is already something to truly love about that.

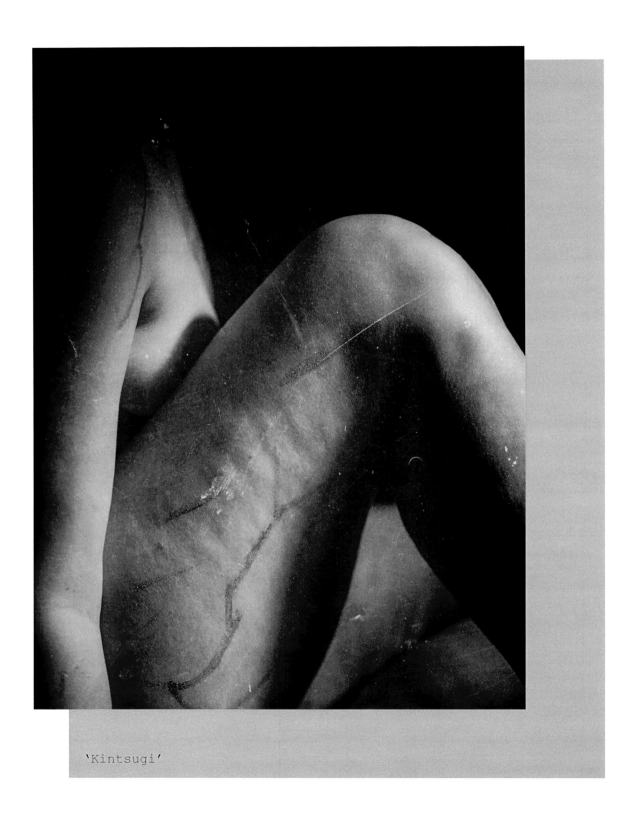

'Kintsugi'

-We Are All A Beautiful Mess-

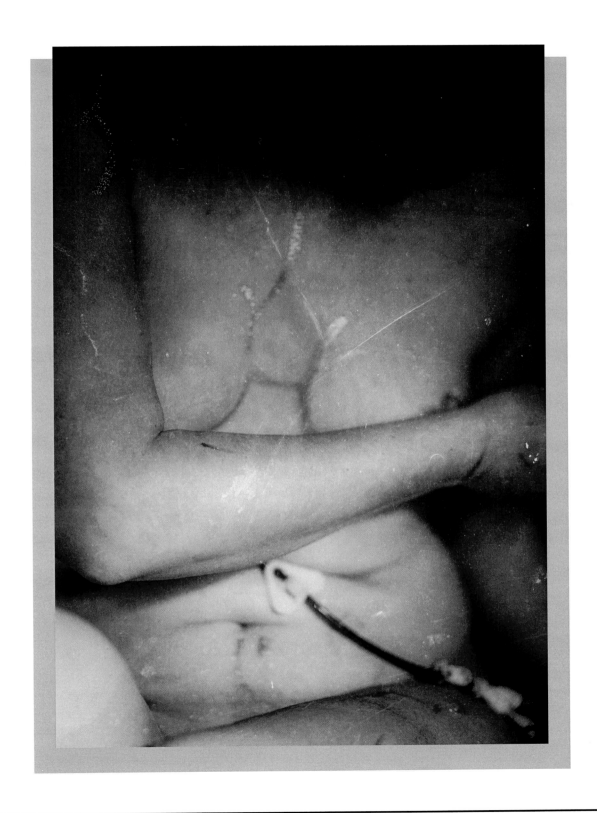

Wabi-Sabi and Bathroom Tiles

-We Are All A Beautiful Mess-

Wabi-Sabi and Bathroom Tiles

'Bathroom Tiles'

-We Are All A Beautiful Mess-

Wabi-Sabi and Bathroom Tiles

'Bath of Blue Tears'-
Painful days lead to tears, cry it out and start again.

-We Are All A Beautiful Mess-

'Yūgen' - The beauty in human sadness.

Daybreak

Sit with me until the day breaks,
Sit with me until then.
Hold me tight until the day breaks,
Let me know I have a friend.
Hold my hand when the day breaks,
Watch the light wash over me.
You give me hope until day breaks,
In these lonely nights of misery.

'Daybreak'

Wabi-Sabi and Bathroom Tiles

'Stranger'

-We Are All A Beautiful Mess-

'Broken'

Wabi-Sabi and Bathroom Tiles

'Normal 1'

-We Are All A Beautiful Mess-

'Normal 2'

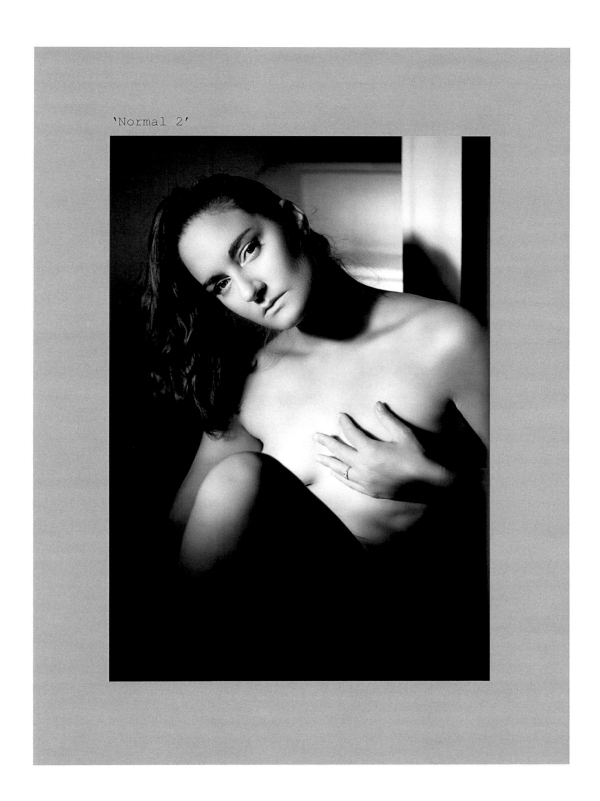

Wabi-Sabi and Bathroom Tiles

Have no fear of perfection, you'll never reach it.

– Salvador Dalí

-We Are All A Beautiful Mess-

Epilogue

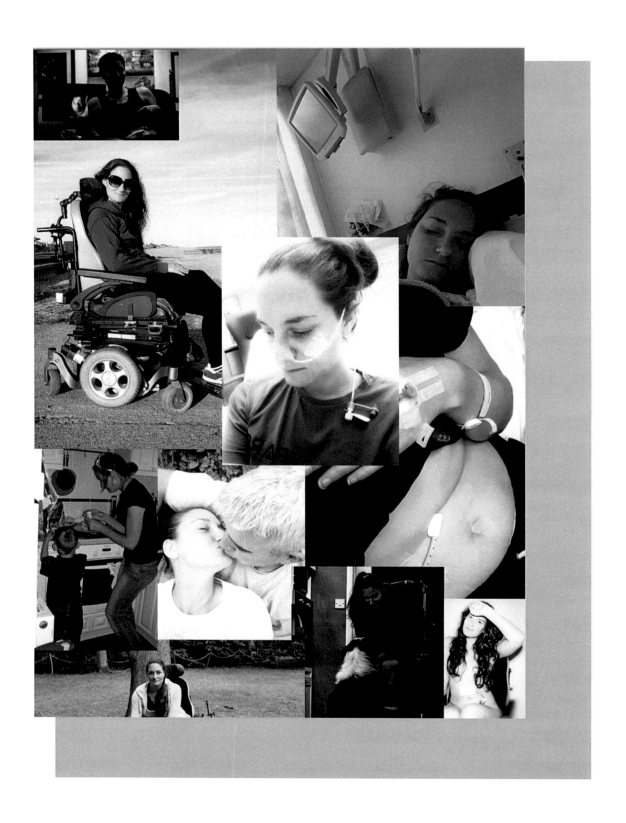

-We Are All A Beautiful Mess-

Snapshots and family life

Now thirty-seven, ten years since my diagnosis of
muscular dystrophy, I am studying to qualify as a counsellor so
I can offer fine art self-portrait photographic sessions as a
therapeutic approach to helping other people who find themselves
in a similar situation to myself.

*"I already know what giving up feels like.
I want to see what happens when I don't."*

-Neila Ray

www.jemmemdart.com